Questions about m

Why do I have eyebrow

Eyebrows are **essential** – they keep water and sweat out of your eyes.

Eyebrows also help with **communication**. What do these eyebrows say?

3

Why is my nose itchy?

Occasionally, tiny specks of things like dust will make you itch. The itch sends information to your brain that something is wrong. The instruction it sends is: *scratch*!

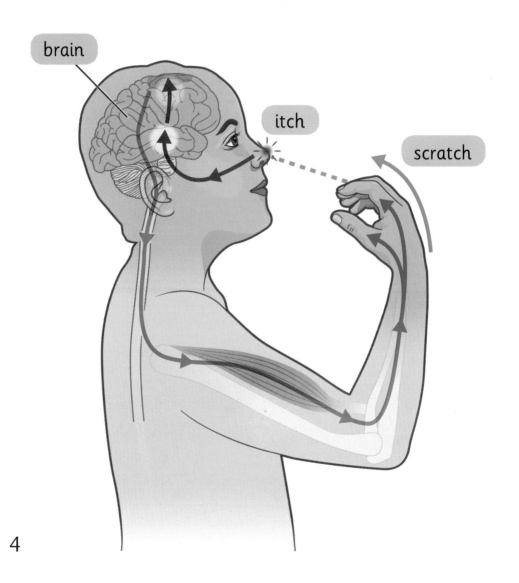

brain

itch

scratch

5

Why am I dizzy?

Your sense of **balance** comes from tiny tubes of liquid inside your inner ear. As you move, the liquid moves, sending messages to your brain.

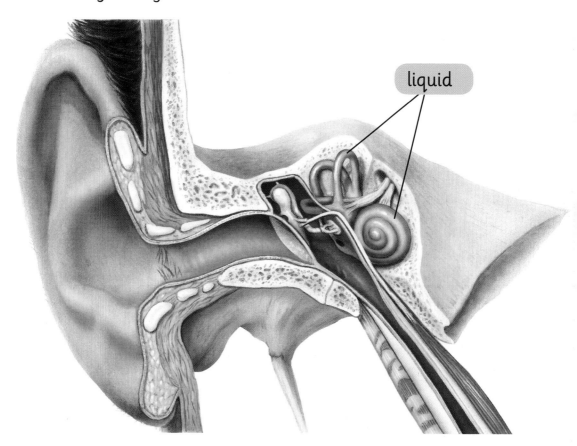

liquid

If you spin, then stop, the liquid in your inner ear is still in motion. Your brain feels confusion – and you feel dizzy.

7

Questions about animals
Why do bats hang upside down?

Most bats' wings aren't sufficiently powerful for take-off from the ground. Bats need a high place to launch from. Hanging upside down is ideal, because a bat can position its wings, then let go and fall into flight.

A bat can eat 3,000 insects in a single night.

9

Why do elephants have such big ears?

Big flappy ears help to keep elephants cool. Body heat **circulates** around their ears and escapes into the air. Hot ears mean a cool elephant!

Elephants also use their ears to signal. Ears spread wide mean *keep your distance!*

11

What colour is a polar bear?

The hairs of a polar bear's fur are actually transparent, and hollow like drinking straws. Their appearance is white because of how they trap light.

Underneath all that fur, polar bears have black skin, because this helps them soak up heat from the sun. So polar bears are white *and* black.

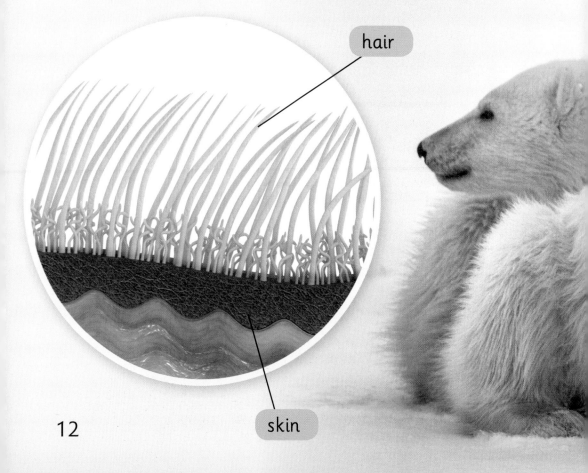

hair

skin

Questions about the earth

Why is the sky blue?

Sunlight is a mixture of all the colours in a rainbow.

You can see all the colours in sunlight using a garden hose.

When sunlight hits the earth's **atmosphere**, it scatters.
Blue light is one of the colours that scatters and **deflects**
most, bouncing down to the ground – and into your eyes,
so the sky looks blue.

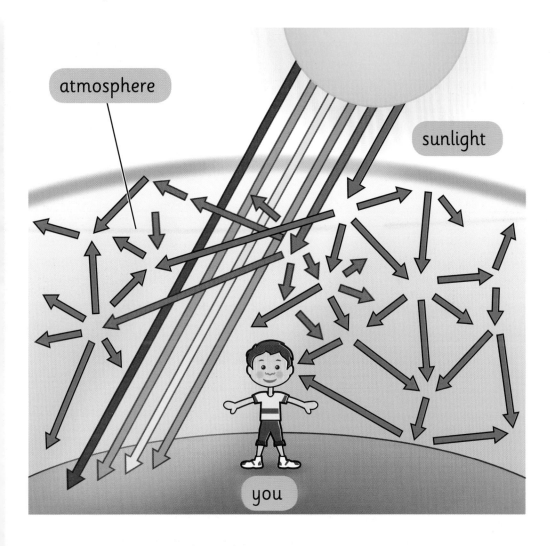

atmosphere

sunlight

you

What makes the wind blow?

The air is always in motion. In hotter places, the air rises. When the air gets cooler, it descends. The wind is just the air mixing and swirling as it heats and cools.

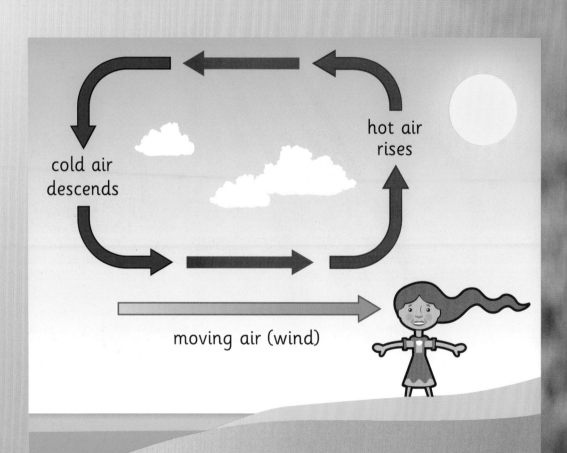

cold air descends

hot air rises

moving air (wind)

How high is the sky?

To reach the middle of the earth, you would have to tunnel down 6,500 kilometres! The sky is not so high. Just 11 kilometres up, there isn't **sufficient** air to breathe, and there are no more clouds or weather.

That's why!

So many big questions, and we've only just begun. What will your next question be?

Glossary

atmosphere	the air around the earth
balance	the feeling of being steady
circulates	travels around
communication	getting and sending messages
deflects	changes the direction it is moving
essential	necessary
sufficient	as much as is needed

Index

The questions

About me

About animals

About the earth

you

After reading

Letters and Sounds: Phases 5–6
Word count: 518
Focus phonemes: /n/ kn /r/ wr /s/ sc c ce /sh/ ti si ci
Common exception words: of, to, the, into, are, so, do, one, our, their, because, water, many, move, eye
Curriculum links: Science: Living things and their habitats/Animals, including humans
National Curriculum learning objectives: Spoken language: listen and respond appropriately to adults and their peers; Reading/Word reading: apply phonic knowledge and skills as the route to decode words, read accurately by blending sounds in unfamiliar words containing GPCs that have been taught, read common exception words, read words containing taught GPCs and –s, –es, –ing, –ed, –er and –est endings, read words with contractions and understand that the apostrophe represents the omitted letter(s); Reading/Comprehension: develop pleasure in reading, motivation to read, vocabulary and understanding by discussing word meanings, linking new meanings to those already known

Developing fluency

- Your child may enjoy hearing you read the book.
- You may wish to take turns to read a page, or share reading out fact boxes.

Phonic practice

- Help your child to practise reading words with suffixes. Ask your child to read each of these words, firstly without and then with the suffix added:

  power   powerful
  play   playful
  care   careful
  mouth   mouthful

- Ask your child if they can think of any other nouns we add the suffix '-ful' to. (e.g. hopeful, helpful, painful)
- Now practise reading words that demonstrate different ways of writing the /sh/ phoneme. Support them as they sound out the following words and then blend the sounds together:

  communication   confusion   sufficient